Questions
God Asks

Questions God Asks

Dick Bernal

Treasure House
An Imprint of
Destiny Image
P.O. Box 310
Shippensburg, PA 17257

"For where your treasure is
there will your heart be also." Matthew 6:21

ISBN 1-56043-780-4

For Worldwide Distribution
Printed in the U.S.A.

Treasure House books are available through these fine distributors outside the United States:

Christian Growth, Inc. Jalan Kilang-Timor, Singapore 0315	Successful Christian Living Capetown, Rep. of South Africa
Lifestream Nottingham, England	Vision Resources Ponsonby, Auckland, New Zealand
Rhema Ministries Trading Randburg, South Africa	WA Buchanan Company Geebung, Queensland, Australia
Salvation Book Centre Petaling, Jaya, Malaysia	Word Alive Niverville, Manitoba, Canada

Contents

Introduction

How many times a day are we asked questions?

What time is it?

Does this tie go with my suit?

What do you want for dinner?

Can you help me with my homework?

Is the report ready?

Questions and questioning are a big part of our lives. Some questions are more important than others, such as:

What college should I go to?

Will you marry me?

Should we buy this house?

Is this the career I really want?

What should we name the baby?

How well I remember cramming for tests in grade school, high school, trade school, and, especially, Bible school. A demand was going to be placed on my ability to remember certain facts and information meted out by my instructors. I remember thinking, "I'll be graded! My parents will know how well I am doing." Staying in the labor union was dependent upon my test scores. And Bible school—now that was a challenge, especially for a man who wasn't raised in church. I am told we can blame the Greeks for the concept of testing.

Apparently centuries ago, certain experts discovered that human beings retain more when they are put under pressure to respond to certain inquiries. But as clever as the ancient Greeks may have been, they were not the originators of the art of questioning. It was God Almighty who began the practice early in His relationship with man.

Let's pause for a minute to ponder this amazing fact: Why would God Almighty ever have to ask a question anyway? Isn't He omniscient—that is, all knowing? You tell me. Okay, then why would this all-knowing Being have to extract information out of us puny, fragile humans with our finite mental capabilities? Is it because He needs the information? Or could it be that our Awesome Creator is wanting us to listen to our own answers, to think about our replies? Our Heavenly Father is in the business of provoking us, prodding us, correcting us, and chastening us, which is all designed to lead to our ultimate good. He judges so He can deliver!

God's desire for man is heaven, not hell. So He asks serious, life-changing questions. His questions are often eternal in nature, direct and to the point. And He asks them without hesitation.

The questions recorded in the Bible that God asked certain individuals concerned matters of the utmost consequence in their lives. In this booklet, we will look at the historical backdrop of the questions we have chosen, and we will consider the spirit of the question. Would God ask us the same questions today? Would He deal with you or me any differently than He did with Adam, Moses, Elijah, Jonah, or any of the other humans He tried to reach, to bless, and to use for His divine purpose?

Let the test begin!

Chapter One

Where Are You?

Then The Lord God called to Adam and said to him, "Where are you?" Genesis 3:9

God's first words to the first sinner were, "Where are you?" Had God lost Adam? Was this some ancient rendition of hide-n-seek? I don't think so!

Obviously God knew of Adam's physical whereabouts, but He was asking a heart-searching question. Sin, disobedience and rebellion had separated Adam from a holy God, and as a consequence he was no longer allowed to dwell in the garden of God.

Fear had entered the hearts of Adam and Eve.

Fear has torment.

Fear drives us away from God.

Fear causes one to hide in the dark.

Fear causes us to cover our own mistakes.

But notice the first gospel message.

Where are you sinner?

I'm calling out to you.

I'm looking for you.

I still love you.

Already the Good Shepherd is out seeking His first lost sheep.

But notice His approach. God doesn't make any promises of restoration until He first sees if He will get an honest answer. God resists the proud, but gives grace to the humble.

Where are you in relationship to Me?

Where is your heart?

Where are your desires?

What is your greatest need?

Why are you afraid of Me?

Who told you you were naked?

Adam was still able to hear the voice of God. Yes, sinners can hear Him—the voice of God speaks in their conscience, convicting so He can convince. What a striking contrast to Calvary, where Jesus took upon Himself the sins of the world and cried out, "My God, My God, where are You?"

Once a sinner grasps the heart of our Heavenly Father, he will run to God in his sin with an open and honest confession on his lips, knowing God is faithful and just to forgive, to cleanse, and to lovingly restore.

Again, let's take another look at the divine approach. Notice that God isn't hasty to judge sin. He isn't running toward the sinner, sword unsheathed to smite.

No! A thousand times no!

God doesn't choose to stalk His prey in the night. At the first break of daylight He doesn't speedily avenge Himself. High noon passes. The afternoon goes by. But in the early evening, in the cool of the day, He comes walking.

He comes calling.

He comes seeking.

Son, daughter, where are you?

Sin stifles, numbs, kills and slowly puts one to sleep.

But God's grace startles.

God's grace shocks.

God's grace awakens us to righteousness.

Let us turn our attention to ourselves.

Where are you?

Where am I?

Right now, this very moment, am I in His hand? Are you? Are we in His plan? Is He really the Lord God Almighty? Is He my God? Is He your God?

Where are you in relationship to Truth? Is the Bible your daily guide? Or have you, like the masses, conjured up your own personal set of rules?

Do you have a homemade morality?

Situation ethics?

Are you following popular beliefs?

Are you running with the crowd?

Where are you?

Are you seeking God and His will for your life? Or is He still searching in the garden of your soul for you—His lost little sheep?

Chapter Two

Where Is Your Brother?

Then the Lord said to Cain, "Where is Abel your brother?" He said, "I do not know. Am I my brother's keeper?" Genesis 4:9

Cain had just murdered Abel. Cain had become outraged because his brother's righteous offering had been accepted by God while his thoughtless one had been rejected. It is interesting that the first murder ever recorded was over an offering.

Let us note that there is a grain of truth in Cain's reply to God. Generally some measure of truth clings to every lie. Satan himself wields truth if it can be used to seduce and ensnare. The grain of truth is that no one can live another person's life for them. Each of us is responsible for our actions before Almighty God. And no, I can't save you, but you can care enough to witness to me.

The story of Cain and Abel is a picture of cool, calculating impudence. This is a picture that has been seen far too often over the passing millennia. It is a picture of selfishness, greed, anger, bigotry and loss.

Cain did not fear God.

He was openly defiant.

He was arrogant in his denial.

He had a hard heart.

He asked the question, Am I my brother's keeper?

God watches how we treat each other.

One of the greatest tragedies of our day is the lack of concern for the well-being of others. So many have come to a place where their love for creatures on a level far below that of man has captured their fancy.

If Jesus died for all of humanity, then you and I must have a sense of concern for all people. If God lives in us, we have a responsibility to be our brother's keeper.

What crosses your mind when the evening news comes on? Portrayed vividly before you are...

The starving children of Africa.

The riots of southern California.

The tragedy of AIDS.

The calamities of Southeast Asia.

Does your soul burn with compassion? Do you pray for the victims?

Do these things provoke within you a desire to give out of your resources to alleviate suffering? Or do you quickly turn the channel? Is your attitude, "Hey, I have my own problems. What is it to me anyway? Do I look like the Good Samaritan?" Or is your attitude, "I'm really concerned"?

I have personally witnessed the poverty of India. My family and I have visited the slums of Beijing, China. I've walked the ghettos of Guatemala, Mexico, and the Philippines. Our brothers and our sisters are everywhere. It is hard for me to pass a beggar in Hong Kong, Korea, Israel, or Europe without stopping and doing what I can to help. Am I naive? Am I foolish? Am I a sucker? Think what you will—I must be about my Father's business. We are instructed to feed and clothe the poor, and to help carry one another's burdens.

Recently in my hometown of Morgan Hill, California, I stopped to minister to a man who appeared to be homeless. His face was racked with pain and misery. He was obviously an alcoholic, lost and confused. When I spotted him, he was looking into the window of a donut shop, and the owner was sending him away. I approached the man and asked if he wanted something to eat, or perhaps a cup of coffee. He seemed startled and he just looked at me. I reached for a five-dollar bill. "Here, God bless you," I told him. I smiled at him and started to leave. He called out to me and asked, "Why did you do that?" I replied, "I have the money and you need it. God bless you."

One doesn't have to travel to the four corners of our planet to find a brother in need. We *are* our brother's keeper!

Chapter Three

Why Are You Laughing? Is Anything Too Hard for the Lord?

Therefore Sarah laughed within herself, saying, "After I have grown old, shall I have pleasure, my lord being old also?" And the Lord said to Abraham, "Why did Sarah laugh, saying, 'Shall I surely bear a child, since I am old?' Is anything too hard for the Lord?..." Genesis 18:12-14a

Abraham and Sarah were both way beyond the age to produce a child. But God had made a promise to Abraham that Sarah would have a son. God wants us to believe His Word—no matter what it looks like.

One old sage wrote, "The incongruity between a divine promise and the sphere of its fulfillment is temptation to unbelief." Doubt, presumption and supposition are by far the greatest sins of the believer. Our belief systems are full of generalizations. We hold fast to a historical Jesus. We claim the Bible as our holy book of absolutes. We thrill at the miracles in the four Gospels. We're proud of Paul, Peter, and John. But like Sarah, when it comes our turn to stand on a promise, to believe for our miracle, we automatically start taking inventory of the "why nots."

I'm an old lady.

Abraham is an old man.

I'm barren. I always have been and always will be.

Sarah, is anything too hard for God? But when it comes to me, I have to admit I have strong faith for others, for those in our church family, for my wife, for my children. But for me?

Over the years, many trusted friends, men and women of God, have shared valuable words of wisdom and encouragement with me. They have told of things to come in my life and ministry. They have shared amazing things, wonderful, sometimes scary things. In my heart I too have sometimes laughed. How could this be? I know me. Why would God Almighty use me in such a way? Yet, when those things would come to pass, I would no longer shake my head in unbelief and wonderment.

Is anything too hard for God?

We're talking about the God of the Bible, the tested, tried, and proven God of the ages. He is not a lifeless, useless, out-of-step God of some dead religion. He is the living God.

The God of the Bible is not the mystical, ethereal deity of the New Age. He is not the cruel, vengeful deity of the

Islamic zealots. Neither is He the traditional God of Western Christianity, on leave from miraculous interventions on man's behalf. He is God Almighty, the One who is above all others. So we must believe that He is and that He is a rewarder of those who diligently seek Him.

Jesus is both the cornerstone and the stumbling block...

He takes us from earth to heaven.

He takes us from fear to faith.

He takes us from doubt to belief.

He takes us from shame to honor.

He takes us from anger to peace.

He takes us from pain to healing.

Is anything too hard for God?

Chapter Four

Shall I Hide From You What I Am Doing?

And the Lord said, "Shall I hide from Abraham what I am doing, since Abraham shall surely become a great and mighty nation, and all the nations of the earth shall be blessed in him? For I have known him...." Genesis 18:17-19a

Abraham and God were in covenant relationship with each other. God was about to intervene in the affairs of Sodom and Gomorrah and decided to tell His friend Abraham what He was doing. Think of it: a friendship where secrets are shared, where intimacy and concern are developed.

To many, God is a mystery—a great, dark secret.

Have you ever listened to a famous person trying to explain God; a person of talent, fame, wealth, education, or power, who is nonetheless spiritually illiterate? No one stumbles more greatly than the "wise man" who knows not God.

Many people love designer products. They have a need to keep up with the new, the fashionable, the trendy.

Have we designed our own God?

A God who adapts Himself to our experiences?

A God who adapts Himself to our whims?

A God who adapts Himself to our desires?

A God who adapts to our beliefs?

Man did not create the true God, though many men have created their own gods in their own minds. Many find it much easier to relate to a god fashioned within one's own heart, by one's own thoughts.

But Christians worship the living God.

We worship the true God.

Who is like unto thee, O Lord?

Is it possible to have a friendship with the Most High God? A working relationship? Intimate fellowship? This is one of the great wonders of Christianity. God isn't just some absentee landlord extracting monthly rent from a group of earthly tenants. He isn't some angry old super Being, all too ready to mete out punishment on the disobedient.

He is our Father and the lover of our souls. Yes, He is our Lord, Savior, Healer, Deliverer, Provider, Judge and much, much more. But let us never lose sight of the wonderful truth that He is also our friend. He is a friend who sticks closer than a brother. He is a friend who tells us what we need to hear, not just what we want to hear. He is a friend who loves at all times.

Chapter Five

What Is in Your Hand?

So the Lord said to him [Moses], *"What is that in your hand?"* Exodus 4:2

God wanted Moses to lead His people out of Egypt and back into the Promised Land. But Moses didn't feel qualified.

God visited Moses, His chosen agent of deliverance, in a very peculiar way. He came to him in a bush that burned, yet wasn't consumed. Out of this bush He assigned Moses a seemingly impossible task. He was to go to Pharaoh, the most powerful man in all of Egypt, and tell him, "Let loose of your free labor force, the children of Israel."

When God first beckoned to Moses, he replied, "Here I am, Lord." After Moses heard God's orders, he responded, "Who am I?" Many people want to please God, that is, until He demands the impossible, the absurd, or the mind-blowing. The Lord has a way of shaking us out of our security, our comfort zone. Moses responded, "Who am I that Pharaoh should obey me, or even believe You sent me. He is not a believer in You anyway! And what about the people I am supposed to help? What makes you think they will believe me?" Moses pleaded for help. But God responded with a question, "What is that in your hand?"

Is it a rod?

Is it a stick?

Is it a staff?

Could it be a piece of old wood I have had for decades?

What does that have to do with this awesome task?

Look at it again, Moses. What is in your hand? Just a simple piece of wood, Lord, why? With that rod and with faith in Me, you will point My people to their destiny; you will part the Red Sea; and you will strike an ordinary rock and water will gush out. That which is in your hand is little, but put it in My hand and it will become much.

What is in your hand that seems so mundane, so ordinary, or so natural. What is it that you haven't given to God? Here are some examples of ordinary things God used to work mighty miracles:

A knife like Abraham's.

The jawbone of a donkey like Samson's.

A slingshot like David's.

Oil and flour like the widow-woman's.

A lunch of five fish and two loaves like the little boy's.

A fishing net like Peter's and John's.

What is in your hand? Can it be used by God to bless this sick and dying world. A woman in the Book of Acts gave her sewing needle to God. This seemingly insignificant act got her raised from the dead. (See Acts 9:36-43)

Years ago I was a construction worker erecting buildings, bridges, office complexes, and the like. God saw that I knew how to construct, pioneer, and lead, so he took my natural abilities and put them to His use in His Kingdom. He helped me build one of the largest churches in the Bay Area.

What is in your hand?

What is your talent?

Can you sing?

Can you play an instrument?

Can you teach?

Can you encourage?

Can you clean?

Can you make money?

Can you act?

Can you cook?

What is in your hand that God can use for His greatness?

Chapter Six

Why Are You Here?

And there he went into a cave, and spent the night in that place; and behold, the word of the Lord came to him, and He said to him, "What are you doing here, Elijah?" 1 Kings 19:9

Most of us at one time or another have asked ourselves the question, "What am I doing here? I shouldn't be here." It is one thing to ask yourself that question, but it is something different all together to have God speak it to your conscience.

Elijah had just experienced the most triumphant moment of his life and ministry. He had single-handedly defeated Baal's influence over God's people.

A nation repented.

A wicked king was embarrassed.

Jezebel was enraged.

But instead of celebrating this great victory and basking in the afterglow of winning, Elijah became fearful. His life was being threatened by the king's wife. Instead of trusting

God he fled in panic. Where was his faith? Where was his courage? He became depressed and suicidal, and he hid himself in a cave. God came to Elijah and asked: "What are you doing here? You don't belong in a cave. I didn't call you to hide from your problems. There is work to be done." Elijah answered, "But, Lord, I have been so zealous for you, and look where it's got me."

Could we at times be confusing our own zeal with that of the Lord's. God doesn't always run at record-breaking speed. Adrenalin and caffeine may *feel* like the anointing, but they are not. How many times have we seen zealous Christians end up far from God because He didn't respond just the way they thought He should? We sometimes seem to think that we are on some kind of holy merit system, racking up sales for the Almighty. We sprint and we pace. And so we find ourselves off course, out of sync.

What am I doing here?

Why am I living here?

Why am I working here?

Why am I ministering here?

Why am I hanging out here?

I would rather be in the furnace with Jesus than at a resort with the devil. We may be able to flee from peril, from our calling, from duty, but we can never flee from that still small voice.

Why are you doing this?

What are you doing here?

Chapter Seven

Who Corrects God?

Moreover the Lord answered Job, and said: "Shall the one who contends with the Almighty correct Him? He who rebukes God, let him answer it." Job 40:1-2

How dare we censor divine intervention? Job was under the impression that bad things happen only to bad people, not to the righteous. But then he found himself under severe satanic attack. He lost virtually everything: his wealth, his health, his children, and his social standing. Job became indignant, even a bit self-righteous. He knew much *about* God, but he didn't *know* God.

The Lord asks Job many questions in Job 38 which reveal God's omnipotence.

"Where were you when I laid the foundations of the earth?"

"Have you commanded the morning since your days began?"

"Have you entered the springs of the sea?"

"Have the gates of death been revealed to you?"

"From whose womb comes the ice?"

"Can you bind the cluster of the Pleiades?"

"Can you send out lightnings?"

These questions reminded Job of who was in command!

How we dream our own dreams and plan our own plans! What is our life outside of God's will? A war broke out in heaven eons ago and continues today, bringing opposing forces together in the lives of each of us.

We are at times perplexed.

We are at times confused.

We are at times sorrowful.

We are at times grieved.

We are at times fearful.

We are at times under siege.

But heaven is watching. Our paths are ordered of the Lord. Our cause is not hidden from the Almighty. To ignore struggle is to expose ourselves to disappointment. The joy of the Lord keeps us strong, even in the face of what looks like disaster.

Job ended up feeling small. His ignorant criticisms soured in his mouth. How many of us question God's infinite wisdom? The modern liberal mind is at enmity with its Creator.

It saves animals and kills babies.

It dictates its own code of morality.

It calls gay what God calls an abomination.

How long will man compete with God's righteous judgments? May we all place our hands over our mouths. May our presumptions be rebuked. God gives grace to the humble, but he resists the proud.

Chapter Eight
Who Will Go?

Also I heard the voice of the Lord, saying: "Whom shall I send, and who will go for Us?" Then I said, "Here am I! Send me." Isaiah 6:8

Isaiah had just seen the vision of visions, the Lord high and lifted up! He had gazed at strange angelic creatures who sang, "Holy, holy, holy is the Lord of hosts." Looking up into the magnificent glory caused him to look down into his own pitiful soul. He responded, "Woe is me, for I am undone! Because I am a man of unclean lips." (Is. 6:5a)

How our little lives fall short when compared to the glory of the Almighty! Isaiah got just a glimpse of it and said, "Ouch! I am a mess, a wretch, vile and base." He then looked out at the rest of his people and said, "I dwell in the midst of a people of unclean lips; for my eyes have seen the King, the Lord of hosts." (Is. 6:5b)

Isaiah saw God and he saw himself. He then turned and looked at the people and saw that their need for God was just as great as his.

Who will tell His story and testify of His undying love?

How well is the soul of your neighbor?

How close to death is your mom or dad?

Dare I share my faith with my friends?

Where are the ministers of reconciliation?

Isn't this an army of volunteers?

We fight for and declare the truth. If we don't, "isms" creep in.

We turn people from darkness to light.

We turn people from sickness to health.

We turn people from sadness to joy.

The world perishes under the curse of sin and death. God's will is that no one be destroyed. How will the masses ever hear of His wonderful love? The Lord cries out, "Who will go for Us?"

Here am I Lord, send me!

Chapter Nine

What Do You See?

Moreover the word of the Lord came to me, saying "Jeremiah, what do you see?" Jeremiah 1:11a

Jeremiah is one of the most fascinating prophets of the Bible.

He was young.

He had low self-esteem.

He was fearful.

God seems to take pleasure in taking misfits and using them for His glory. The Bible says that those things which are foolish in man's eyes can best reveal the wisdom and glory of God.

God was trying to get Jeremiah to see something.

Something prophetic.

Something violent.

Something cleansing.

Something judging.

Something necessary.

The Word of the Lord came to this young man. He was instructed to:

Root out.

Pull down.

Destroy.

Build.

Plant.

Prophecy is revolutionary. It is stirring and energetic.

God's truth rearranges. Violence is sometimes used as a means to bring about righteousness. One can never negotiate with evil. Jesus brought a sword, not détente. God will clear all obstacles to bring about His plan. A little criticism is healthy if it brings about truth.

What was God trying to get Jeremiah to see? What does He want you and me to see? Jeremiah saw a budding almond branch, which symbolizes the wakeful and watchful attitude of God in human events. He saw the boiling pot of impending doom. Jeremiah saw clearly. Will he speak of what he saw? Will he warn the people?

What is God showing us? Do we see a sick and dying world? Do we see decay and moral bankruptcy? Do we see a Savior? Do we see hope?

Are we warning sinners of impending judgment or are we afraid of their faces?

Can we handle mocking from lost family members?

Dare we lose a friend over our convictions?

Having eyes to see, do we see?

Having a mouth to speak, do we speak?

How important is our reputation when Jesus did not have one?

Then Jeremiah said, "Ah, Lord God! Behold, I cannot speak, for I am a youth." But the Lord answered the young prophet, "Do not say, 'I am a youth,' for you shall go to all to whom I send you, and whatever I command you, you shall speak." (Jer. 1:6,7)

No more excuses; what do you see?

Chapter Ten

Can We Walk Together?

Can two walk together, unless they are agreed? Will a lion roar in the forest, when he has no prey? Will a young lion cry out of his den, if he has caught nothing? Will a bird fall into a snare on the earth, where there is no trap for it? Will a snare spring up from the earth, if it has caught nothing at all? If a trumpet is blown in a city, will not the people be afraid? If there is calamity in a city, will not the Lord have done it? Amos 3:3-6

With God, where there is smoke, there is fire. His threats are not empty ones. God has chosen to associate with human beings, many of whom are stiff-necked and rebellious. Many of us argue, fuss, and complain. We see no judgment in sin. We disconnect ourselves from God as we would a boat trailer from our car. But God doesn't give up easily:

> He watched us in Egypt.
>
> He walked us through the Red Sea.
>
> He camped with us in the wilderness.

He fought for us in Canaan.

He rained on us in the desert.

He caused our crops to grow.

All He desires is our gratitude, our worship, and our affection.

How far do we dare stretch His patience, His mercy and His grace?

Will it tear?

Just a little more rebellion. One more fling. So far, so good. I'm sowing to the flesh, yet where is the reaping? Perhaps I will be the first to get away with murder?

The clock is ticking. If there is thunder, there will also be flashes of lightning. If the lion is roaring, He will also rend. If the light is red, stop!

How long can a person drive up a one-way street going the wrong direction and not crash? How long can he tread water in the middle of the ocean?

God's judgments are designed to deliver. He came to seek and to save those who are lost. Man was not intended for hell, but paradise. Can't we walk with Him? Aren't we tired of kicking against the goads? He always warns of evil long before it comes. As a hurricane approaches we board up our windows. Thank God for satellites. We're insured to the hilt against fire, earthquake, flood, tornadoes, you name it. The commercials tell me to "Get MET," "You're in good hands with Allstate," or "Get a piece of the rock."

But, what about God?

He is eternal life insurance.

He is eternal fire insurance.

He is eternal storm insurance.

Sign on the dotted line...right across your heart.

Chapter Eleven

Why Are You Angry?

So he [Jonah] *prayed to the Lord, and said, "Ah, Lord, was not this what I said when I was still in my country? Therefore I fled previously to Tarshish; for I know that You are a gracious and merciful God, slow to anger and abundant in lovingkindness, One who relents from doing harm. Therefore now, O Lord, please take my life from me, for it is better for me to die than to live!" Then the Lord said, "Is it right for you to be angry?"* Jonah 4:2-4

Jonah was intensely angry. A spirit of anger had taken hold of him. Why was he so overwrought? Was it the Ninevites? Jonah had prophesied their doom which he felt they deserved. Let them all die in their sin!

But they believed his warning.

They listened.

They repented.

Here was a preacher who was mad because the people responded positively to his sermon!

Holy passion is good and righteous anger is necessary. But Jonah became mean spirited. His reputation was on the line. His anger was sinful, selfish and arrogant. God had graciously intervened, and His mercy had found an object to which it could attach itself. Masses of humanity were spared. Rejoice Jonah! "No, I will not!" Jonah became so angry that he wished himself dead. He pitied a gourd that had a short life more than he pitied human beings!

Why are you angry?

God was merciful to you in your sin; should he not be merciful to others?

Anger unchecked becomes a flame and it makes life unbearable.

We see rage.

We see jealousy.

We see revenge.

We see murder.

We see insanity.

Let us be slow to anger, slow to speak, slow to react. The wrath of man does not produce the righteousness of God.

Our society has an attitude problem. How many temper tantrums can we throw?

How silly much of our anger really is!

My favorite team lost.

My birthday was overlooked.

My tire went flat.

My plane was late.

The best laid plans go astray. Let us not trust in earthly good. All flesh is as grass. Life is a test and a struggle. May the winter of your anger give way to the spring of eternal joy.

Chapter Twelve

What Are These High Places?

"What is the transgression of Jacob? Is it not Samaria? And what are the high places of Judah? Are they not Jerusalem? Therefore I will make Samaria a heap of ruins in the field, places for planting a vineyard; I will pour down her stones into the valley, and I will uncover her foundations." Micah 1:5b-6

High places were an abomination to God. They were shrines erected to the gods of wood, stone, silver or gold.

They were places of false worship.

Places of idol worship.

Places of demon worship.

Dumb idols.

False deities.

God is a jealous God. The land was dotted with high places, and God gave the people specific instructions to remove and destroy them. Root them up!

I have seen the fruit of idolatry during my ministry in India, China, and Latin America.

I have seen the poverty.

I have seen the confusion.

I have seen the disease.

I have seen the death.

Incense is burned.

Candles are lit.

Prayers are offered.

Money is given to graven images infested with evil spirits.

How unthinkable! Why do people worship their own tormentors? God detests high places because they build strongholds in people's minds. Paul tells us that God's weapons can pull these strongholds down. He also tells us that we wrestle not against flesh and blood, but against evil princes and powers, against rulers, authorities, and wicked spirits in high places. (see Ephesians 6:12)

What high place or high thing in your life exalts itself over God's Word? We can become addicted to more than just alcohol, nicotine, caffeine, or drugs in general:

What about our jobs?

What about our hobbies?

What about our families?

These can all become modern-day high places.

Remove the barrier.

Tear down the wall.

Burn the altar.

"You shall have no other gods before me," says the Lord. As my dad used to say, "Why settle for hamburger when there is steak on the plate?"

Chapter Thirteen

You Looked for Much, Yet It Has Become Little. Why?

Now therefore, thus says the Lord of hosts: "Consider your ways! You have sown much, and bring in little; you eat, but do not have enough; you drink, but you are not filled with drink; you clothe yourselves, but no one is warm; and he who earns wages, earns wages to put into a bag with holes." Thus says the Lord of hosts: "Consider your ways! Go up to the mountains and bring wood and build the temple, that I may take pleasure in it and be glorified," says the Lord. "You looked for much, but indeed it came to little; and when you brought it home, I blew it away. Why?" says the Lord of hosts. "Because of My house that is in ruins, while every one of you runs to his own house. Therefore the heavens above you withhold the dew, and the earth withholds its fruit." Haggai 1:5-10

Some things never change. We ministers are always struggling to convince the crowd that God is number one. We have building programs. We have stewardship campaigns. Ugh! Please, Lord, must we? There is no greater challenge to a church than building God's house. Here come the critics. There go the tightwads.

"We're behind you 100%, pastor." Some are so far behind me that I've lost sight of them. "Oh, well." The faithful still dream. Someday, Lord. "I'd like to help you preacher, but you see my money is tied up." Hmmm! Could it be, sir, that you are the one bound? We look down our evangelical noses at all the "isms," but what about materialism? Am I preaching, "Lack is best? Poverty is godliness?" No! It is not either/or, but both and more.

God does prosper. He loves to bless. Abundance is at the heart of why Jesus came. But it all must be tempered with selflessness, divine duty, and establishing God's covenant on planet earth. Today, churches are being turned into theaters, coffee houses, offices, even mosques. Old, beautiful places of former glory. What happened? Was it compromise, worldliness or secularism?

What are our priorities?

We struggle with the temporal versus the eternal,
the natural versus the spiritual.

Excuses versus conviction.

Our interests versus His glory.

And the war rages on.

God is left to search for a people who will put Him back on the throne of their lives. Come, let us build Him a house of honor.

Chapter Fourteen

Did You Really Do It For Me?

Say to all the people of the land, and to the priests:
"When you fasted and mourned in the fifth and
seventh months during those seventy years, did you
really fast for Me—for Me? When you eat and when
you drink, do you not eat and drink for yourselves?
Should you not have obeyed the words which the
Lord proclaimed through the former prophets when
Jerusalem and the cities around it were inhabited
and prosperous, and the South and the Lowland were
inhabited?" Zechariah 7:5-6

How much of our religion is pure? Are we undefiled
in our Christian service? I just came off an eighteen-day
Daniel fast. I'm going to do another one later this month
for nineteen days; thirty-seven days is a tithe of the year
to the Lord. I was bragging to a brother the other day
about how much weight I had lost. I heard a whisper,
"Was it for Me?"

I love to eat and fasting is not one of my favorite pastimes. To give up meat, bread, cheese and desserts is a chore, but the rewards are great.

"Is this the fast I have chosen?"

The hypocrites draw attention to themselves. They pray and fast for public praise. They constantly remind you of their holy walk with God, yet the Lord looks behind the mask. How many other Christian duties minister to the flesh, the ego? How many do little more than shore up our self worth?

Lord, I want a big church.

Son, is it for Me?

Lord, I want to go on television.

Son, is it for Me?

Lord, I want....

Chapter Fifteen

Where Is My Honor?

"A son honors his father, and a servant his master. If then I am the Father, where is My honor? And if I am a Master, where is My reverence? says the Lord of hosts to you priests who despise My name. Yet you say, 'In what way have we despised Your name?'" Malachi 1:6

The Book of Malachi deals with the deception of backsliding. These wayward, rebellious Israelites were so deceived they didn't even know how far they had strayed. "How have we strayed?" they asked. Backsliders can't see the forest for the trees. They turn the truth into a lie and believe the lie.

I'm not so bad.

Who says it is sin?

But look at all the good I've done.

How do I know the Bible is God's Word?

The Bible is too rigid, too constricting. I'll make my own rules.

The Lord is not pleading here with new converts who, in their immaturity, stumble. He is dealing with priests, seasoned veterans, old pros. Leaders come under a stricter judgment.

Greater condemnation.

Stronger rebuke.

Count the cost.

Here the Lord is appealing to family feelings. The figure of fatherhood is used. Sentiments, duties and obligations are described.

A son honors his father. A servant honors his master. What is the difference?

A father-son relationship is based on love and affection. A master-servant relationship is based on obligation.

Blood ties the one. Duty ties the other.

We are God's children. He loves us like a good father.

The greatest revelation of God to me was that of Father.

He is a good Father.

He is a just Father.

He is a patient Father.

He is a correcting Father.

He is a loving Father.

He is a tender Father.

Notice again in verse 6, God asks, "If I am a Master, where is My reverence?"

Could He be saying, If you don't love Me, at least respect Me? The fear of God is the beginning of understanding. It is absolutely foundational. We must get back to the basics. Back to peg one.

If you don't go to church,

If you don't pray,

If you don't worship,

If you don't give,

If you don't serve

out of affection and joy, at least begin at the starting gate. If you can't yet see Him as Father, see Him as Master.

See Him as Creator.

See Him as Judge.

See Him as God Almighty.

He has a divine claim on all of us. He owns the patent. We are His invention. From dust to glory.

Lord, we honor You.

Father, we love You.

God Almighty, we fear You.

Chapter Sixteen

Will a Man Rob God?

Will a man rob God? Yet you have robbed Me! But you say, "In what way have we robbed You?" In tithes and offerings. Malachi 3:8

It is absurd to think that we would rob God. Robbers are bad people. They are low-lifers, scum, dregs of the earth. Away with them all. Lock them up. Throw away the key. God certainly is speaking to the vagabond, the outcaste. He couldn't be asking one like you or me such an amazing question could he?

God always deals with us honestly and firmly, yet with abundant love and mercy. His Word cuts, yet heals. It divides while uniting. Convicting one's soul of sin is no easy task in these days. Yet a man will not seek pardon if he is not convicted of his sins.

Who is good? None, but God.

How would we decent sorts rob God? Break into a church and take the sound system? Sue a fellowship for some seeming infraction? Hold up a preacher at gun point?

Actually, according to Scripture, the one who robs God may sit in church Sunday after Sunday; he may say amen to every sermon point the preacher makes; he may smile at the other parishioners; and he may even be involved in lay ministry.

But, he robs God by holding back his tithe, God's holy portion, the tenth.

He is robbed of love and obedience.

He is robbed of true worship.

For the most part, thieves operate in the dark, in shadowy places. They break in through the back door, going behind their victim's back. Yet, God is robbed openly, right before his face in broad daylight. How brazen are we creatures of the dust!

Are we really so ungrateful for the life God has given us?

I remember as a child taking a dollar out of my mother's purse. I felt so guilty I couldn't sleep. Dare I keep back from my Heavenly Father that which is holy to Him? God's promises come with a warning label. You do this and I will do this. But if you don't, I won't. God speaks by commandment, not suggestion.

I am not bound by the law of the tithe, but by the spirit of it. Father Abraham locked me into a spiritual reality when he gave a tenth to Melchizedek centuries before the Mosaic law was given. He gave out of faith, not duty. He gave in sincerity, not just obedience. His gift came from a willing heart, not a guilty one. He wasn't giving to get, but to worship. The obedience of giving tithes and offerings has been one of the most important principles I have incorporated into my walk with God.

If things are not going well in your life, check and see if you are lacking in the area of giving. The Lord said in the next few verses in Malachi, "Bring all the tithes into the storehouse...and try Me...if I will not open for you the windows of heaven and pour out for you such blessing that there will not be room enough to receive it. And I will rebuke the devourer for your sakes." (Mal. 3:10-11a)

God challenges us to prove Him now.

Chapter Seventeen

Who Do Men Say That I Am? Who Do You Say That I Am?

When Jesus came into the region of Caesarea Philippi, He asked His disciples, saying, "Who do men say that I, the Son of Man, am?" So they said, "Some say John the Baptist, some Elijah, and others Jeremiah or one of the prophets." He said to them, "But who do you say that I am?" And Simon Peter answered and said, "You are the Christ, the Son of the living God." Matthew 16:13-16

A day doesn't pass that this question is not hashed and rehashed a thousand and one times. The world is full of both experts and fools. Opinions are half priced these days. Everyone's got one or two. As a child growing up in a non-Christian home, Jesus was an enigma to me. Who was He? He got me out of school for two weeks in the winter to celebrate His birth and for one week in the spring to honor

His resurrection. "He must be pretty important to get me out of school," I thought. But why did He have to be killed? I wondered. Didn't people like Him?

Some say He is an angel.

No, He is a prophet.

Perhaps a magician.

He is a curse word.

A Jewish zealot.

A dreamer.

A liar.

Some say He is God's Son.

Some say He is a Savior.

Some say He is the soon coming King.

But, what and who is He to me? Why do I need to be saved? If He's the answer, what is the question? My soul is sick, you say. My spirit is dead. I need help? Perhaps a new life? Maybe I should go to the library and check out some self-help books. Not good enough? Okay, what do I need?

Regeneration.

Open-heart surgery.

The old man put to death.

A personal resurrection.

The infilling of God's Spirit.

A new lease on life.

A new source of power.

Focus.

Meaning.

Destiny.

Eternity.

I'll take it all!

Who do you say that I am? You are the Christ, the Son of the living God.

Chapter Eighteen

Why Do You Call Me Lord?

"But why do you call Me 'Lord, Lord,' and do not do the things which I say?" Luke 6:46

Jesus asks us hard questions. If He is really Lord of our life, there will be no doubt about our total allegiance to Him and His will.

Two things we must consider—being and doing.

Who really is Jesus?

> Prophet
> Teacher
> Son of God
> Son of Man
> Messiah
> Guru
> Angel
> Fanatic?

So we've decided He is Lord.

He is the Son of God.

The Word made flesh.

The incarnate God.

All divine—All human.

We come to His church. We read His words. But, do we do His will?

Have we confused church membership with divine calling?

Has our will remained sovereign?

Character comes forth in conduct. Meditation on His Word must lead to activism. Converts are plentiful, workers are few. Christianity is to be as practical as it is spiritual.

Every tree is known by its fruit.

We reap what we sow.

A right heart leads to a right walk.

Dare we call Him Savior and Lord, and never attempt to obey Him?

Has the fear of failure derailed our destiny?

Ceremony and ritual can never replace caring and sharing.

That which I receive from the Lord, I must give.

Dig deep, friend. Build a strong and sure foundation. Piety should lead to conviction and determination or it is useless religion. Paul was freed to become a bondslave to Christ. Not all who call Him Lord shall enter into eternal life.

A true Christian is in the process of becoming Christ-like.

A true believer believes.

Prayer is talking and listening.

Obedience is better than sacrifice.

Why do we call Him Lord?

Chapter Nineteen

Who Touched Me?

And Jesus said, "Who touched Me?" When all denied it, Peter and those with him said, "Master, the multitudes throng You and press You, and You say, 'Who touched me?'" Luke 8:45

The crowd was pressing in on all sides. Many curious hands were touching Jesus, poking Him, pulling on Him, and patting Him on the back. But one hand touched Him differently. It belonged to a suffering woman, a woman who had been sick for many years and who was broke and desperate. She was on a virtual suicide mission. According to the law, she was unclean. A woman with a bleeding condition was not to be out in the public without issuing the warning, Unclean! Unclean! Yet she made her way through the crowd.

This woman had heard of Jesus. He could heal people. He turned no one away. He showed favor to all who came to Him. "If I could just touch Him" was the cry of her heart. Faith and hope overrode her fear and despair. "Will my desperate action be rewarded?" she wondered. "Is there a place in His heart for me?"

"Who touched Me?" the Lord suddenly asked. "Lord, hundreds are touching You," the disciples responded. "Look around, they all want to feel you." "No," said Jesus. "One has touched me with need; I feel power leaving me. A demand was placed on My anointing."

Faith had been revealed. The woman received what she desired. Desperate faith was rewarded. She was congratulated by the Lord.

How do we touch Him?

With our membership in a local church?

Through our ministers or priests?

Perhaps through our wife's prayers?

Maybe our offerings are touching Him?

Should we be a little more adventurous?

Should we be a little more intimate?

Should we be a little more passionate?

He doesn't want a handshake or a pat on the back. He desires us to grab hold of all of Him and never let go. In Him is all that we need.

Touch Him today!

Chapter Twenty
Who Is My Neighbor?

And behold, a certain lawyer stood up and tested Him, saying, "Teacher, what shall I do to inherit eternal life?" He said to him, "What is written in the law? What is your reading of it?" So he answered and said, "You shall love the Lord your God with all your heart, with all your soul, with all your strength, and with all your mind, and your neighbor as yourself." And He said to him, "You have answered rightly; do this and you will live." But he, wanting to justify himself, said to Jesus, "And who is my neighbor?" Then Jesus answered and said: "A certain man went down from Jerusalem to Jericho, and fell among thieves, who stripped him of his clothing, wounded him, and departed, leaving him half dead. Now by chance a certain priest came down that road. And when he saw him, he passed by on the otherside. Likewise a Levite, when he arrived at the place, came and looked, and passed by on the other side. But a certain Samaritan, as he journeyed, came

where he was. And when he saw him, he had com-
passion. So he went to him and bandaged his wounds,
pouring on oil and wine; and he set him on his own
animal, brought him to an inn, and took care of him.
On the next day, when he departed, he took out two
denarii, gave them to the innkeeper, and said to him,
'Take care of him; and whatever more you spend,
when I come again, I will repay you.' So which of
these three do you think was neighbor to him who
fell among the thieves?" And he said, "He who
showed mercy on him." Then Jesus said to him, "Go
and do likewise." Luke 10:25-37

This passage is the story of a Jewish businessman on his
way from Jerusalem to Jericho. He falls among thieves who
rob him and nearly kill him. Life is full of such painful experiences. The well-traveled path down to Jericho was
famous for such violent incidents. It was nicknamed "the
bloody path."

As the Jewish man lay bleeding in the street, his life was
slowly seeping out of his body. Certainly he prayed to
Jehovah God for help. He heard footsteps. Could it be that
his prayers were heard? He looked up and it was a priest,
a "man of God." Glory hallelujah! But wait! He passed by
on the other side of the street. He must have been in a hurry.
He had already done his religious duty for that day, and
now he was late for dinner. The wounded man heard more
footsteps. A Levite! Another reader of holy writ. Will he
help? The Levite stopped and sized up the situation. He
shook his head. He moved on. Was all hope lost? Not yet

friend! Here comes a Samaritan. A Samaritan? The one despised by the Jew? The hatred between these peoples ran deep. To the Jews, Samaritans were accursed dogs. Undoubtedly the Samaritan would rejoice at the condition of the Jew; yet the eyes of this man were full of compassion.

He's helping me. He's ministering to me. He's caring for me. Why? I can't repay him, the thieves took all my money. What is in this for him? Certainly he too is in a hurry. This is costing him time and money. But even in the face of danger the Samaritan paused to lend a helping hand.

Like the road to Jericho, life has many dangerous curves to it. The daily newspapers tell us day after day of the misfortunes of others. The evening news on television brings regular reports of human misery, even death itself, right into our living rooms. Have we become calloused? Have we lost sensitivity to the pain of others? Can we still be touched by the plight of victims living thousands of miles away?

As I write this chapter, my son Adam and I are stuck in New Delhi, believing we can catch a plane to Hyderabad and eventually arrive in Guntur, our destination. We are surrounded by poverty. Our waiter just told us he makes the equivalent of thirty U.S. dollars a month. He asked for a pair of shoes. He is not a Christian; he is a stranger. There are millions of stories like his in this vast nation, yet he is my neighbor. He is asking for help. It is five a.m.; it is noisy, and I am very tired. I am also irritated at the airlines, yet I will look in my suitcase for a pair of shoes or whatever else I have that he may need.

Are you challenged by the question, "Who is my neighbor?"

Who do you feel bound to help?

Is it the one whose skin color is the same? The one whose language is the same? Those who are members of your same club? Or, could it be just another human being who is in need?

Or is it family, close friends, perhaps a member of your church?

Remember, man is not an island and was not created to be one. Human beings function best when cross pollinated. We are to touch and be touched by others. Jesus gave prominence to the practical, which under His direction, is always helping others. Let us set a high standard of duty, especially when it comes to dealing with our fellow man.

Chapter Twenty-One

How Much More Shall Your Heavenly Father Give the Holy Spirit to Them That Ask?

If a son asks for bread from any father among you, will he give him a stone? Or if he asks for a fish, will he give him a serpent instead of a fish? Or if he asks for an egg, will he offer him a scorpion? If you then, being evil, know how to give good gifts to your children, how much more will your heavenly Father give the Holy Spirit to those who ask Him! Luke 11:11-13

A normal natural Father can never turn away from the pleadings of his children, if he can possibly help it. One of the great joys of life is not only to give our children necessities, but to grant them their dreams as well. Christmas morning is always a treat, especially when there are wide-eyed children anxiously waiting to open their gifts.

How much bigger is the heart of our Heavenly Father? Notice the sequence:

Bread and fish—staples.

An egg—a luxury in the days of Jesus.

The Holy Spirit—the ultimate blessing.

We have not because we ask not. Right prayers, right answers. Selfish prayers, no answers. Would you give your infant a sharp knife or a poisonous serpent? No, of course not. Would our Heavenly Father injure those who humbly ask for the supply of their needs?

Can we get a glimpse of His grace?

Do we yet grasp true faith?

Has justification by the blood been lost in our contemporary sermons?

We are asking the baby boomers the wrong questions.

Do you believe in God?

Do you believe the Bible is the Word of God?

Why don't you go to church?

Their real questions are: Will God help me? Is he interested in my dilemma? Yes, I believe in God, but how do I get in touch with Him? Help me, someone!

We fear the great Judge in the sky, the "Man Upstairs." Dare I ask for something good? Will I be disappointed?

In our zeal to be independent, have we abandoned the need to ask of our willing and able Father?

If we ask for salvation, it shall be granted.

If we ask for power, it will come from on high.

If we ask for wisdom, it will not be withheld.
If we ask for strength, it comes with joy.
If we ask for direction, He will light our path.
"How much more...?"

Chapter Twenty-Two

Have You Counted the Cost?

Or what king, going to make war against another king, does not sit down first and consider whether he is able with ten thousand to meet him who comes against him with twenty thousand? Or else, while the other is still a great way off, he sends a delegation and asks conditions of peace. So likewise, whoever of you does not forsake all that he has cannot be My disciple. Salt is good; but if the salt has lost its flavor, how shall it be seasoned? Luke 14:31-34

As Jesus began attracting a large following, He became concerned that the motives of the people were not based on fact, but only speculation. Ministry certainly can be exciting and adventurous, but for the most part it is thankless hard work. Following Jesus Christ never has been a stroll through the park. Relationships are instantly put at risk. Family, friends and even employers begin to wonder. We pastors love large crowds, good offerings, and sharp programs, all in the name of Christ; yet at times our egos get a little too wrapped around our true calling.

We must have quality before quantity.

We must make disciples out of converts.

Jesus had a gift of trimming back the forces. Paul seemed to excel in this area as well. One pastor told me, "I'd rather have two hundred workers than two thousand lookers."

Do we leaders warn enough?

Is sin still mentioned in our modern self-help society?

Is there still cause to mention the blood?

I have seen far too many false starts and pipe dreams— too much untempered zeal. The Bible is full of blinking lights: caution, slow down, look both ways. We dangle prosperity and health in front of the curious to compel them to join our fellowships, but are we preparing them for the onslaught of demons sent to discourage them? We sell hard to fill the altars on Sunday morning, but are they leaving with the real picture?

We live in an age of quotas.

We live in an age of charts.

We live in an age of big budgets.

We live in an age of demographics.

We compete to impress. Yet, Gideon became used to the three hundred. God Himself had the first church split and lost a third of His congregation. Pruning is necessary for growth. Jesus said, "He who loves father and mother more than Me is not worthy of Me." (Mt. 10:37)

Ouch! That is rough!

But Jesus, I am pressured by obligation. What will my friends say? I am naturally shy. Lord I will follow you, but *first* let me go and...

> make money,
>
> finish college,
>
> prepare my family.

Sorry, if I can't be first, I won't be second.

> The time is short.
>
> The clock is ticking.
>
> The workers are few.
>
> The eternal rewards are great.

Think about it!

Count the cost!

Chapter Twenty-Three

Do You Want to Be Made Well?

Now a certain man was there who had an infirmity thirty-eight years. When Jesus saw him lying there, and knew that he already had been in that condition a long time, He said to him, "Do you want to be made well?" The sick man answered Him, "Sir, I have no man to put me into the pool when the water is stirred up; but while I am coming, another steps down before me." Jesus said to him, "Rise, take up your bed and walk." And immediately the man was made well, took up his bed, and walked. And that day was the Sabbath." John 5:5-9

Such a silly question. Who wouldn't want to be well, complete, whole? Yet for many, apathy creeps in. Hopelessness sets in. Things will never change. Once bright-eyed people of vision, dreamers, but now paralysis has set in.

Here lies a cripple, pining away next to the pool of hope. The healing water is still in sight, but he has been this way for thirty-eight long years. Would the angel ever trouble the water for me? My insignificance is overwhelming me. If I could just get my body healed, life would be so much better. Right, but sir, what of your soul, your spirit? Would you be made whole?

To you in prison I ask, "Would you rather be pardoned or have integrity of heart?"

To the impoverished I ask, "Would money solve all your problems?"

To the physically sound, the young, the strong I ask, "Is it well with your soul?"

To the rich I ask, "Have you stored up treasures in heaven?"

To the addict, the bound, I ask, "Will you be free to serve?"

Are you one of those who has the ability to serve, but not the willingness? Or are you willing, but not able? Be made whole! But at what price, you ask?

I've worked hard.

I've gained much.

My reputation.

What would people say?

Sometimes we allow our present condition to become an old friend. There is no development more noble than that of one's immortal soul. There is no loftier goal than to let God be the Lord of all. Righteousness, peace and joy await all who choose God's ways. Reconciliation, atonement, absolute forgiveness, holiness, these are more than biblical terms—they are medicine. We take our vitamins, our juices, we obey the doctor's orders and take two pills a day, but are we whole? Paul prayed for the whole man— spirit, soul and body—to be made complete and preserved until the coming of the Lord.

Will you be made whole today?

Chapter Twenty-Four

If I Tell the Truth, Why Do You Not Believe Me?

"But because I tell the truth, you do not believe Me. Which of you convicts Me of sin? And if I tell the truth, why do you not believe Me? He who is of God hears God's words; therefore you do not hear, because you are not of God." Then the Jews answered and said to Him, "Do we not say rightly that You are a Samaritan and have a demon?" Jesus answered, "I do not have a demon; but I honor My Father, and you dishonor Me. And I do not seek My own glory; there is One who seeks and judges. Most assuredly, I say to you, if anyone keeps My word he shall never see death." John 8:45-51

Truth can hurt. Truth can startle. Truth can even frighten certain people. In the passage above we see religious people arguing with Jesus over truth. Truth is designed to liberate, not bind. Man has a deep need for truth. In Psalm 45, we see the King riding off to battle, prosperous because of truth, humility and righteousness. He straps a sword on His thigh. We have a sword in our mouth, the living Word of God.

If we quit defending and proclaiming the truth, "isms" will fill the void. History proves this is so. Jesus is the way, the truth, and the life. His word is absolute truth. Man lies, but God is truth. Communism, Hinduism, Islam, Mormonism, Taoism, Humanism are all laced with gross error. Judaism had its day. Jesus is Truth.

We weep over the world's unbelief, yet what about the unbelief in the church?

Complacent Christians.

Half-hearted preachers.

Sermons lacking compassion.

Services more secular than spiritual.

Double standards.

Jesus set a high standard—"Follow Me!"

The secular at least have consistency in their walk.

"I will not."

"I don't believe."

"I won't go."

Terrible as it is, hell-bound as they may be, at least there is no hypocrisy in their statements. But to hide behind a mask of righteousness, to say "hallelujah" and "amen," and then go and lie against the truth, "My brethren, this ought not to be so."

Yes, the truth convicts.

Yes, it is humbling.

Yes, it pierces.

Yes, I know our reputations are at stake.

But, repentance is sweet.

The truth will set us free if we allow it to. If we live it. If we share it.

Would you be free from the power of sin? The truth declares to the lost, you must be born again.

To the prodigals, Arise, go home to your Father's house.

To the lukewarm, Be baptized with fire.

To the zealots, Let wisdom temper your desire.

We act on our doctor's orders. We trust the prophecies of the newspapers. We repeat things we hear without checking reliable sources. But, we resist the holy Scriptures.

Repentance is more than being sorry. We're all sorry when we get caught. But are we turning from sin? Truth is good. The goodness of God turns the hearts of men away from sin. The New-Agers attack Christianity as a social disease. The truth is, it is a cure, a remedy for man's sin-sick soul. Grace is more than a few words over one's meal.

The lake of fire has not disappeared.

Hell is not a myth.

Time may not be short, but your time could be.

Grasp the truth of God's Word.
Why gamble with your soul?
The dice will eventually come up "snake eyes."
God is not mocked. We all reap what we sow.
There is still time.
Faith lays hold of the promises of God.
Sharpen your sword.
Ride off to battle with the King.
The truth will prevail.

Chapter Twenty-Five
Do You Love Me?

So when they had eaten breakfast, Jesus said to Simon Peter, "Simon, son of Jonah, do you love Me more than these?" He said to Him, "Yes, Lord; You know that I love You." He said to him, "Feed My lambs." He said to him again a second time, "Simon, son of Jonah, do you love Me?" He said to Him, "Yes, Lord; You know that I love You." He said to him, "Tend My sheep." He said to him the third time, "Simon, son of Jonah, do you love Me?" Peter was grieved because He said to him the third time, "Do you love Me?" And he said to Him, "Lord, You know all things; You know that I love You." Jesus said to him, "Feed My sheep." John 21:15-17

How many times has my wife asked me, "Honey, do you really love me?" I would respond, "Of course, darling, you know that I do...don't you?" "Well, you could show me a little more now and then," she replies. "Buy me a rose, hold my hand, call me for no reason except to say, I miss you." Hopeless romantics some women are.

Hopeless romantic is our Lord!

Do you love Me, Dick?

Hey, lighten up, Jesus. I'm working for you, aren't I? I'm serving you. I am preaching Your Word. I am running off to India, China, and Africa converting the lost. "That's nice, son," our Lord replies. But then He asks, "Do you love me?"

Such a short question. Can we give a quick reply? Or best we ponder.

How I love church.

Great people at Jubilee.

Man, I love to read the Word.

I love to preach the Word.

Jesus isn't asking whether we love His things; He wants to know if we love Him. He is very personal, you know. He is intimate, friendly, and concerned. People who love Jesus hate sin. When we do sin, repentance is good and necessary.

Peter sinned against his Lord. He denied Him three times and was asked to confess his love three times. The Lord wants to be sure of our love.

For some, loving can be so difficult. Many have been abused, rejected, divorced, or betrayed. Dare we trust again? Will the Lord hurt me too? No!

He will never leave you.

He will never abuse you.

He will never reject you.

Never!

He is the lover of lovers.

He is a friend who sticks closer than a brother.

Let us return His love. Let your soul soar with praise. Lift up the hands that hang down. Taste and see that the Lord is good.